by Dawn McMillan
illustrated by Meredith Thomas

SCHOOL PUBLISHERS

Printed in Mexico

ISBN 10: 0-15-350655-5
ISBN 13: 978-0-15-350655-0

Ordering Options
ISBN 10: 0-15-350599-0 (Grade 2 On-Level Collection)
ISBN 13: 978-0-15-350599-7 (Grade 2 On-Level Collection)
ISBN 10: 0-15-357836-X (package of 5)
ISBN 13: 978-0-15-357836-6 (package of 5)

3 4 5 6 7 8 9 10   050   15 14 13 12 11 10 09 08

Poor Giraffe had a sore throat.
"I can barely speak," she whispered.

"Let me have a look," said the
zookeeper. "Open wide."

"Goodness," he gasped. "This is
extremely serious! You have spots on the
inside of your neck! You need to see the
doctor. Off to the zoo hospital you go."

The next day, Elephant, Monkey, and
Goat went to the hospital to visit Giraffe.

"How are you feeling this morning?"
asked Goat. "We are lonely without you."

"Is your throat still sore?" asked
Elephant. "We hope you will be well soon."

4

"You look *very* comfortable," said Monkey.
"I *am* comfortable," said Giraffe. "This
bed is extremely soft and the food is fine."

5

When Monkey returned to the zoo, he sat on his hard bed. Suddenly, he thought of a clever plan. He climbed his tree and called to the animals.

"Watch me! I'll perform some tricks! I'll dazzle you with some jokes!"

The animals watched in amusement as
Monkey jumped from branch to branch,
singing silly songs and making faces.

"Oh, you are hilarious!" giggled
Elephant. "Don't stop!"

"You are so witty," shouted Goat.

7

Monkey smiled to himself. Everything was going according to his plan. "Now watch me swing all the way to the ground!" he shouted.

When Monkey reached the ground, he toppled over and grabbed his leg. "Help! I'm injured!" he called. "I have to go to the hospital immediately! I think I've broken my leg!"

At the hospital, Monkey was given an extremely soft bed. He snuggled down and smiled smugly to himself.

The doctor came to examine Monkey.
"Now which leg have you broken?" she
asked.

"My left leg!" cried Monkey.

"Hmmm," said the doctor, "your left leg
seems perfect to me."

"Then it must be my right leg," cried
Monkey. "It's so sore, and I'm very confused."

"Monkey," said the doctor, "I don't believe that you have injured your leg at all. You've been tricking us! It is never good to trick others into thinking you are hurt. What will happen if you really hurt yourself someday?"

12

"I'm sorry," Monkey whispered. "When I saw Giraffe in a soft hospital bed, I just had to try one for myself."

"Giraffe is going home today, and you can go home, too," smiled the doctor. "Perhaps the zookeeper can make your bed softer."

Later, when Monkey and Giraffe returned to the zoo, Monkey called to all his friends.

"I have to admit that I didn't really hurt myself," he said. "I only pretended to be hurt so that I could try out the soft beds at the hospital. I'm sorry! I know I was wrong."

"We forgive you, Monkey," said all the animals. "Now tell us another funny joke!"

Think Critically

1. What was Monkey's plan?

2. How do you think Monkey felt when he had to tell the doctor the truth?

3. What was the difference between how Giraffe and Monkey ended up in the hospital?

4. What did Monkey do after he and Giraffe returned to the zoo?

5. If you were a zookeeper, what animal would you like to look after? Why?

 **Social Studies**

Write a Paragraph In the story Monkey tricks the other animals but they forgive him. Write a paragraph about how Monkey could have behaved better. Tell whether you think he learned his lesson.

School-Home Connection Tell a family member about *Monkey Business*. Explain how Monkey changed during the story.

Word Count: 473